WILLIAM

DUKE OF CAMBRIDGE

ANNIE BULLEN

Prince William, Duke of Cambridge, more than any other member of the Royal Family, is regarded as a modern individual, someone who has lived and worked alongside ordinary people. He is grounded in the history, tradition and value of the monarchy while also understanding the need to make the Royal Family, of which one day he will be head, a thoroughly up-to-date organization.

Son of the Prince of Wales and the late Princess Diana, His Royal Highness Prince William Arthur Philip Louis, Duke of Cambridge, Earl of Strathearn, Baron Carrickfergus, Royal Knight Companion of the Most Noble Order of the Garter is the full title of the man seen by many as a bright hope for the future.

Prince William, second in line to the throne, has been used to the spotlight of media interest at home and abroad since boyhood. His every move – from school, to university, to training in the armed forces and, especially, his romance and marriage – has been the focus of intense public interest.

As Prince William celebrates his 30th birthday, the good wishes of a nation, looking up to him as their future King, go with him.

DATES & EVENTS

1982 Prince William born on 21 June at the private Lindo Wing of St Mary's Hospital, Paddington, London.

1982 William is christened on 4 August, his late great-grandmother's birthday.

1985 William's first day at school; the decision to send him to a nursery school broke with royal tradition.

1991 The young Prince William undertakes an early public engagement when he accompanies his parents, Prince Charles and Princess Diana, on a visit to Llandaff Cathedral to celebrate St David's Day.

1995 Prince William, as 'William Wales', goes to Eton College, in Berkshire.

2000–01 William undertakes a 'gap year', which includes projects in Belize, Chile and Mauritius.

2001 The Prince goes up to St Andrews University to study Art History; he meets fellow student Catherine Middleton.

2002 In September, William and Catherine with two friends move into a student house in Hope Street, St Andrews.

2003 William's 21st birthday party is held at Windsor Castle; Catherine Middleton is invited. In September he and Catherine share a cottage for their third year at university.

2006 Prince William starts his Army training at Sandhurst, where he receives his commission as a second lieutenant in the Household Cavalry Regiment in December.

2007 In March, Prince William starts five months training with his regiment at Bovington Camp in

Dorset. In April he and Catherine part – but the split lasts only a couple of months; by June the couple are reconciled.

2008 In January, the Prince begins an intensive four-month flying course at Cranwell to learn how to handle fixed-wing aircraft and helicopters. He graduates from the course in April.

2010 William graduates from an advanced helicopter flying course, receiving his wings from his father, the Prince of Wales. He starts work experience at RAF Valley with the helicopter Search and Rescue team.

2010 In September, he starts work at RAF Valley as a co-pilot with the Search and Rescue team.

2010 On 16 November, Clarence House announces William's engagement to Catherine Middleton.

2011 In February, William is made a Colonel in the Irish Guards. He attends his first public engagement with his fiancée when they name a new lifeboat in Anglesey. The following day they visit St Andrews University for its 600th anniversary.

2011 In March, William and Catherine make an official visit to Northern Ireland. A week later the Prince travels to Australia and New Zealand, for an official visit, to show solidarity with the people who had suffered, respectively, from terrible flooding and a massive earthquake.

2011 On 29 April, William marries his long-time sweetheart Catherine Middleton at Westminster Abbey. The couple receive the titles Duke and Duchess of Cambridge from Her Majesty The Queen.

2011 In July, the Duke and Duchess of Cambridge make official visits to Canada and the United States.

A PRINCE
IS BORN

A proud father, tenderly holding his newborn son, stood outside St Mary's Hospital, Paddington, London, on 23 June 1982. Prince Charles, heir to the throne, held the child who would also one day be King. The baby, just 36 hours old, a tag on his tiny wrist identifying him only as 'Baby Wales', scarcely stirred as cameras flashed and journalists shouted questions. 'The birth of our son has given us both more pleasure than you can imagine,' said a delighted Prince.

Prince William Arthur Philip Louis of Wales entered the world at 9.03 p.m. on 21 June in the private Lindo Wing of the hospital. He was driven with his parents to Kensington Palace, which would be his home for the next 15 years.

William's mother Princess Diana adored her baby son. She nicknamed him 'Wills' and 'Wombat', two names that have stayed with him. The first test came just a few weeks after his birth, when she and Prince Charles were to tour Australia. Traditionalists, assuming that Diana would leave her baby at home, were surprised when she insisted that William should go too. The world approved, as pictures were shown of William's nanny Barbara Barnes carrying him from the aircraft on the other side of the world.

William's great-grandmother, the late Queen Elizabeth the Queen Mother, celebrated her 82nd birthday on 4 August 1982, the day chosen for the christening of the six-week-old Prince. William, wearing the Royal Family's Honiton lace christening gown, was baptized by Dr Robert Runcie, the then Archbishop of Canterbury, in the Music Room at Buckingham Palace.

Right: Charles and Diana, Prince and Princess of Wales proudly show off their baby son, Prince William Arthur Philip Louis in June 1982.

THE
EARLY DAYS

Diana, determined to be a 'hands-on' mother as far as her royal duties allowed, was helped by nanny Barbara Barnes with William's daily care and companionship. Perhaps the young William was a little too indulged – by the time he was three and his baby brother Prince Harry, a year old, William's natural exuberance sometimes gained the better of him and it was clear that some discipline was necessary. This was one of the reasons why Prince Charles and Princess Diana decided that William should break with the royal tradition of lessons at home with a governess, and start nursery school.

Thus it was that on 24 September 1985 a cluster of reporters and photographers jostled for position outside a small private nursery school in Notting Hill Gate, with cameras trained on one small boy dressed in red shorts and a red check shirt.

The transition from the rarefied atmosphere of the Palace, where he was the centre of his mother's and nanny's attention, might have been hard, but it has stood William in good stead, teaching him to socialize and work with others.

Parents of other children at Mynor's Nursery School in Notting Hill Gate were contacted by Princess Diana, who apologized in advance for any disruption caused by William's attendance. There was the obvious press attention,

Left: Prince William shows off a finger puppet made at his first day at nursery school in September 1985.

Right: Wearing his new blue cap, William smiles on the day he starts at Wetherby pre-prep school.

the presence of his bodyguard and new classroom windows, made of bullet-proof glass.

The young Prince stayed at Mynor's Nursery for two years before moving to nearby Wetherby pre-prep school, where there was scope for his aptitude for sport and enjoyment in taking part in school activities. It was at this time that a new nanny, Ruth Wallace, arrived at Kensington Palace to teach her young charge not only self-reliance but also the importance of consideration to others.

Both William and, later, his younger brother Harry, moved on to become boarders at Ludgrove School in Berkshire, where William excelled at sport, becoming captain of both the 2nd XI hockey and 3rd XV rugby teams and one of the school stars at clay pigeon shooting in 1994, when he was 12 years old. He won the school's Junior Essay Prize in 1992.

Prince William's birth and early years saw many changes to the traditional upbringing of the 'heir presumptive' (an heir, other than the first, in line to the throne). He was born in hospital, rather than at the Palace, sent to nursery school and saw much more of his parents than most royal children.

Above: Headmaster Gerald Barber and his wife Janet greet William, as he arrives to board at Ludgrove School in September 1990.

Right: Sporty William enjoys a game of tennis at Ludgrove. The young Prince shone on the sport's field, where he was one of the best shots and captained both the rugby and hockey teams.

Above: Princess Diana and her sons Prince William (right) and Prince Harry enjoy a water ride at Thorpe Park; seen with them is Thorpe Park director Colin Davison.

In late 1992 a solemn-faced Princess of Wales visited Ludgrove, the Berkshire school where both her sons were boarders. She had something serious to tell them. She and the Prince of Wales, their father, were to separate. Diana wanted to talk to the boys herself, before the news was officially announced in the House of Commons. Harry, probably too young to understand the implications, looked dazed, but William, desperately upset, could not hold back the tears. The boys and Diana were to continue living at Kensington Palace, but they would still spend time together with their father, in London, and at Highgrove, the Prince of Wales's country house in Gloucestershire.

It was at this time a new figure entered William's life – the cheerful, sporty Alexandra Legge-Bourke, known to all as 'Tiggy'. Tiggy was taken on as an assistant private secretary in Prince Charles's household, but her real role was to be a companion to the young Princes.

Tiggy loved the boys and saw that they had fun. She devised outings for them, taught them to ski and accompanied them on riding and fishing expeditions. She ensured that they enjoyed civilized family dinners together when they stayed at Highgrove. William stayed close to Tiggy during school and university days, asking her to be his guest at Eton's 'June the Fourth' celebrations in 1996. Three years later she took both the Princes on holiday to Botswana.

If he took part in country pursuits when he stayed with his father, William would also look forward to more everyday entertainment with his mother, who was determined that her sons would have the treats that other children enjoyed. They would visit burger restaurants and theme parks, or spend time watching films together.

Tiggy Legge-Bourke (now Mrs Charles Pettifer) was brought up on her parents' 6,000-acre (2,428-hectare) country estate, Glanusk, in South Wales, where she learned to ride, shoot and fish. Her mother, the Hon Shân Legge-Bourke, is Lord Lieutenant of Powys and a Lady-in-Waiting to the Princess Royal. Her brother, Harry, was a Page of Honour to Her Majesty Queen Elizabeth II while her son, Tom, was one of the two pageboys at the wedding of Prince William to Catherine Middleton in April 2011.

Left: Prince William and Prince Harry arrive at Zurich in February 1994 for a skiing holiday; also pictured are their father the Prince of Wales, and nanny, Tiggy Legge-Bourke.

Below: William and Harry (left) led by Prince Charles, taking part in the Beaufort Hunt in 1997.

WILLIAM
WALES

Prince William was just nine years old when he carried out his first public engagement. Although he was the focus of intense attention, he seemed quite at ease as he accompanied his parents on a visit to Llandaff Cathedral, Cardiff, to celebrate St David's Day in 1991. From the day he was born, William, like every member of the Royal Family, has had to learn that whatever he does, and wherever he goes, he will always be in the public eye. As eventual heir to the throne, he has had to understand that the job is one for life. A visit to the Principality from which William takes his title was an appropriate introduction to public life, and he cheerfully wore a bright yellow daffodil in his buttonhole.

After the cathedral service he accompanied his mother to Cardiff's City Hall, where they met local dignitaries and a couple of young people dressed as teddy bears. In the afternoon he was rewarded for his good behaviour with a personal tour of the aircraft museum at RAF St Athan in the company of Captain Norman Lloyd-Edwards, the Lord Lieutenant of South Glamorgan. That was William's first official engagement, but during his childhood he accompanied his parents

It was when the young Prince, under the watchful eye of his mother, signed his name in the visitors book at Llandaff Cathedral, that onlookers noticed that he was left-handed.

Below: Prince William, carrying daffodils and the Welsh flag, smiles shyly for the cameras.

Above: Prince William, undertaking his first official engagement in Wales on St David's Day, 1 March 1991 with his mother Princess Diana, is greeted by crowds outside Llandaff Cathedral.

on a number of visits so that he could become used to the public attention that is normal for every member of the Royal Family.

He has inherited not only the Windsor sense of duty but also his mother's easy manner with the crowds, and his own charisma and self-assurance stand him in good stead in all his public appearances.

Princess Diana was the unofficial mascot of the Welsh Rugby team and a fervent supporter, bringing William and Harry with her to international matches at Cardiff's Millennium Stadium. Both boys took pride in learning the words of the Welsh National anthem – in Welsh – so that they could join with gusto in the community singing.

William, like his mother before him, attracts adulation and attention. Tall, fair-haired, blue-eyed and good-looking, he stands out in the crowd and has always received the sort of welcome normally reserved for pop stars. Also, like his mother, he knows how to handle the crowd, chat to well-wishers and seems at ease in any situation.

Above: William, resplendent in black tie, arrives at a movie premiere in London, in aid of his father's charity, The Prince's Trust in 1997.

Below: William greets the crowds gathered to meet him in the Royal Botanic Gardens, Sydney, Australia, during his visit in January 2010.

LIFE AT
ETON COLLEGE

When it was time for William to continue his education, Diana and the Queen Mother were in agreement over the chosen school. This again was a break with royal tradition as the often testing regime of Gordonstoun, the Scottish public school attended by William's grandfather, father and uncles, was eschewed in favour of Eton College, possibly the most famous educational establishment in the world.

The Berkshire college, with its centuries-long tradition of producing self-confident young men and its outstanding educational reputation, was a happy selection. William was pleased not only that many of his friends from Ludgrove would join him, but also that the school was close to Windsor Castle where he could visit his grandmother The Queen for Sunday tea.

The distinctive Eton uniform of black tailcoat, striped trousers, waistcoat and white bow tie was established in 1820, when the whole establishment went into mourning for the death of King George III. When William was elected a member of 'Pop', the elite group of sixth formers at the College allowed to wear waistcoats of their own choice, the more startling the better, he enthusiastically took advantage of this privilege.

Below: William, with the help of his mother Princess Diana, signs the school book at Eton on his first day there in September 1995. Prince Charles and Prince Harry look on.

'William Wales' signed the Eton school book in September 1995, on his first day there. His study-bedroom, in Manor House (where he was the only boy afforded the luxury of a private bathroom), was a cell-like 4m (13ft) x 3m (10ft) with a narrow single bed and, at once, William stamped his own mark on it, putting up a picture of Aston Villa soccer team, and a signed poster of All Saints, his favourite band at the time.

As at Ludgrove, William excelled at sports, enjoying soccer and rugby, and shone especially in the school pool, where he became the 'Keeper of Swimming' – Eton-speak for captain of the swimming team. He also did well academically, gaining three A-levels and winning a place at St Andrews University. First, he decided to see something of the world by taking a gap year.

'June the Fourth' celebrations, marking the birthday of William's ancestor King William III, Eton's greatest patron, herald the start of Summer Long Leave and are always held on the Wednesday nearest to the 4th. Parents and friends attend, to enjoy a cricket match and boating processions.

Right: A cheerful William cuts a dash in his Eton uniform.

Left: An inter-house soccer tournament at Eton in 2000, where William captains his house (Gailey's) team in the semi-final.

Below: Prince William is pictured in his study-bedroom working on his computer, during his final year at Eton.

At William's wedding to Catherine Middleton in April 2011 a special chocolate biscuit cake was served alongside a more traditional wedding cake. This was made at William's request to remind him of special teatimes with his grandmother The Queen, when he was allowed out of school to visit her at Windsor Castle.

IN THE
PUBLIC EYE

T he world was moved by the sight of the two young sons of Diana, Princess of Wales walking slowly, heads bowed, behind her funeral cortège on Saturday 6 September 1997. The boys were at vulnerable ages – William, 15, and his brother Harry, two years younger – when their beloved mother died in a tragic road accident in Paris.

The two were asleep at Balmoral when the dreadful news came through. The Queen and Prince Charles let them sleep on until morning when Charles, calling Harry into William's bedroom, gently broke the news to both of them. The three were very close during that time, father and sons comforting each other as best they could and talking about Diana.

The Princes stayed at Balmoral for a few more days before travelling to London, where William and Harry were astonished by the thousands upon thousands of flowers laid by well-wishers, outside the railings of Buckingham Palace and Kensington Palace. They watched silently as lines of people moved quietly forward, waiting patiently up to 12 hours to sign the books of condolence at Kensington Palace. The day before Diana's funeral, Prince Charles, William and Harry joined the grieving public outside Kensington Palace, thanking people for their tributes and condolences.

The great carpet of flowers, the ranks of solemn mourners and the overwhelming public grief brought home to William just how much his mother had been loved by so many people.

Left: Three grieving Princes gaze at the flowers left outside Kensington Palace in memory of Princess Diana, in September 1997.

Below: Prince William and Prince Harry walk slowly behind the coffin of their mother on 6 September 1997. With them are the Duke of Edinburgh, their uncle Earl Spencer, and their father Prince Charles.

William, as older brother, gave the younger Harry the unqualified support and friendship that he would have needed after their mother's death. Highgrove, the Gloucestershire country home of Prince Charles, was a secure refuge for both boys at this time, where Prince Charles coped admirably with their care after the loss of their mother. When their father married his long-time companion Camilla Parker Bowles, the Duchess of Cornwall, both the young Princes were happy, not only for their father but also because they enjoyed family life with her.

Above: Prince Charles with William and Harry at Highgrove, their home in Gloucestershire, in July 1999.

Right: Prince William shares a joke during a visit to the Pacific Marine Heritage Legacy in Canada, in 1998.

The following day, the autumn sun shone brightly as the coffin, draped with the Royal Standard, carrying the body of Diana, Princess of Wales was borne on a gun-carriage from Kensington Palace to Westminster Abbey. Behind the coffin, walking slowly, were the dark-suited young Princes, their father Prince Charles, grandfather the Duke of Edinburgh and uncle Earl Spencer, Diana's younger brother. The white tulips on the coffin were from William, while a card with the one word 'Mummy' lay on Harry's wreath of white roses.

As the crowd sobbed, the young Princes, wretched inside, kept their emotions firmly under control, showing a maturity and a sense of duty that belied their years.

BRIDGING
THE GAP

William had worked hard at Eton, gaining three A-levels – Geography, History and Biology. Now, before university, he wanted to see something of the world and, like many other students, he decided to take a gap year. Travel, adventure and experience were the criteria for the widening of William's education. His first destination was Belize where he joined the Welsh Guards on exercise in the wet, stifling-hot and humid jungle. He had to learn what to do if bitten by a snake (chop its head off and keep the body to assess the dose of venom received) and how to kill and gut chickens before cooking them over an open fire. Here he slept in a hammock, slung unceremoniously between two trees. He also received instruction in handling semi-automatic weapons, the first time he had used this type of gun, although he was already an excellent shot, having had plenty of practice at home and at school.

In complete contrast to the steamy and uncomfortable jungles of Belize, the soft white sands, blue sea, warm sun and gentle breezes of Mauritius in the Indian Ocean were pure delight. Among the volunteers with the Royal Geographical Society's 'Shoals of Capricorn' marine conservation programme was one 'Brian Woods' who stayed, virtually incognito, for a month. This helper on the island of Rodrigues, 300 miles (482km) south-east of Mauritius, was William Wales who travelled by moped, scuba-dived on the coral reef and spent a little time teaching the rudiments of rugby to local lads.

Left: During his gap year, Prince William helped to build wooden walkways between buildings in the small village of Tortel, in Chile. Materials had to be carried to the building site.

It was while he was in Belize that William received his A-level results – by email from his father. The email, telling the Prince that he had achieved an 'A' in Geography, 'B' in History and 'C' in Biology, was the first that Prince Charles had sent.

Most testing was Chile, which came next, during the cold, wet and miserable rainy season. The first week of this Raleigh International expedition saw torrential rain day and night. The young volunteers, soaked to the skin, had never experienced anything like it.

'Eventually even the tent became wet through; it was saturated ... we became quite demoralized even though we somehow managed to keep ourselves going by singing, telling jokes and stories ...,' said William on his return. But, when the rain stopped, the volunteers moved to the village of Tortel, teaching English to the children, tidying up the neighbourhood and making friends with the locals.

William used paintbrush and saw to strengthen and varnish the exterior of the local radio station and to make a litter bin for the village.

Above left: Smaller carpentry jobs included making wooden litter bins for the Tortel villagers.

Above right: Prince William relaxes in his sleeping accommodation during his stay in Chile.

Right: The Prince enjoys a joke with a student whilst teaching an English lesson in Tortel.

THE STUDENT
PRINCE

William, more than any other future British Sovereign, has experienced 'ordinary' life in many ways. There were no footmen or valets at boarding school and certainly none at university, where a flat share with other students meant helping with the chores, like everyone else. He has, of course, enjoyed the privileges accorded to royalty. Before his marriage, whenever he stayed in a royal residence – Highgrove, St James's Palace in London, Balmoral in Scotland, or Sandringham in Norfolk – he would be woken each morning by a footman bearing a 'calling tray' with a pot of coffee and biscuits. As he opened his eyes, his curtains would be drawn, the radio turned on and clothes laid out by a valet.

There were certainly no servants to make the early morning routine go smoothly when, in September 2001, William Wales went up to St Andrews, becoming one of 6,000 students at Scotland's oldest university.

His first accommodation was in the rambling Gothic co-educational hall of residence St Salvator's (Sallies to its inhabitants), where he tumbled

Left: A casually dressed Prince William arrives at St Andrews University in September 2001 at the start of his course.

William has always accepted the authority of his grandmother Her Majesty Queen Elizabeth II, who laid down ground rules for his sojourn at St Andrews University. He was told he must not smoke, drink only moderately and was never to take any illegal drugs. Nor must he be seen kissing any woman he dated. He was never to ask his bodyguard to leave him alone, even at private parties. The last was a rule that William and all senior members of the Royal Family observe with rigour: never to discuss any member of the Royal Family even with those to whom he had become close.

Above: William studies in the university library during the last year of his three-year course at St Andrews.

Right: The Prince chats to Dr Charles Warren, senior lecturer in Geography at St Andrews.

out of bed in the morning, showered and helped himself to breakfast in the communal dining hall, chatting to whoever happened to be there at the time. He usually opted for fruit and cereals – the healthy choice – but occasionally enjoyed a couple of bacon butties with a mug of steaming hot tea.

Breakfast over, he would join fellow students in the lecture rooms, see his tutor to discuss an essay or, if there was no work on the agenda, stroll into town to buy newspapers and perhaps join friends for a coffee. It was at St Andrews that William met Catherine Middleton with whom he and two other friends eventually moved out of hall to share a flat.

FRIENDSHIP &
LOVE

However outgoing, experienced and well-connected the student, the first few weeks at any university can seem daunting and so it must have been for both Prince William and the pretty dark-haired fresher from Bucklebury, in Berkshire, whose friendship he soon began to value.

Prince William and Catherine Middleton often sat together over breakfast, eaten in the grand ground-floor dining hall of St Salvator's with its stained-glass windows and portraits of Scottish philosophers lining the walls. They discovered a mutual love of the countryside, and had sporting pursuits and swimming in common. At first they were both studying history of art and, by coincidence, their gap years had followed a similar pattern, giving them plenty to talk about.

By the start of their second year, they were part of a group of four friends sharing a flat. The couple were discreet, never touching or holding hands in public, arriving at parties separately and, to the world and the sharp-eyed press, just good friends.

As friendship turned slowly to love, William knew he had found a woman with whom he felt comfortable. She was sporty, sharing his love of the outdoor life, as well as being cheerful, resourceful and creative. They shared a sense of humour: 'She has a really naughty sense of humour, which helps me, because I have a really dry sense of humour. We had a good laugh – and things happened,' he later told the world's press. During their third and final years at university they shared a secluded cottage and, with the help of a tight circle of loyal friends, managed to keep the relationship a secret.

Below: Her Majesty Queen Elizabeth chats to her grandson Prince William after his university graduation ceremony, in June 2005.

But, university days over, the secret was out in the open. William had to fulfil his royal duties, and the press were never far away. When they were spotted on the slopes enjoying a skiing holiday together at Klosters, media attention was intense. No one had seen them behaving as if they were enjoying a close relationship, but they were always out and about together and suddenly Catherine, who had just moved into a flat in central London, found the full glare of the media spotlight on her private life. She managed remarkably well, ensuring that every time she stepped outside her front door she was dressed suitably, wearing make-up and coiffured, in order to face the battery of photographers lying in wait.

It was Catherine who persuaded Prince William not to give up his university course when, in the early days, he decided that Art History was not for him. She was instrumental in ensuring that he carried on studying, later switching his degree to Geography. William gained an upper second in Geography – the highest university honours ever won by an heir to the British throne.

Left: Prince William and Catherine Middleton heading for the slopes on a ski lift in Klosters, Switzerland.

Below: William and Catherine relaxing on the day of their graduation ceremony at St Andrews University.

A WORKING
PRINCE

From the moment of his birth, Prince William's destiny was determined. One day Prince William, the Duke of Cambridge KG, FRS, will be crowned King William V.

Today he is a fully operational RAF Search and Rescue pilot but, although he also has commissions in the Royal Navy and the Army, he can never be ambitious about carving out a permanent career in the armed forces, of which he will one day be the head. Nor will he make his way in a profession. Every aspect of his life has been shaped to ensure that his future role as Sovereign is the predominant factor.

After university William undertook work experience from land management to banking, but, following royal tradition, decided to join the armed forces.

William has always enjoyed an active social life and, in the period after university, he and Catherine celebrated the weddings of friends such as Hugh van Cutsem and Rose Astor, Lady Rose Windsor and George Gilman, and Laura Parker Bowles and Harry Lopes. The couple enjoyed traditional royal pursuits such as race meetings at Cheltenham and Epsom, as well as entertainment at fashionable London nightclubs.

He received his Army commission as a second lieutenant in the Household Cavalry in December 2006 when he graduated from Sandhurst after almost a year at the Royal Military Academy, watched at the passing out parade by his grandmother Her Majesty The Queen, his proud father the Prince of Wales and by Catherine Middleton.

Although Prince William followed his younger brother Harry into the Blues and Royals (the Household Cavalry Regiment) as a troop commander in an armoured reconnaissance unit, his wish to see active service was discouraged, so William trained in both the Royal Navy and the Royal Air Force, winning a commission as sub-lieutenant in the former and flying officer in the latter.

An intensive four-month training course at RAF Cranwell won him his wings, presented to him in April 2008 by his father, a ceremony that was watched, among others, by Catherine. A period with the Royal Navy followed, during which William, on board HMS *Iron Duke* in the Caribbean, took part in a secret underwater mission, helping to foil drug smugglers.

Although William cannot serve in combat zones, he was able to train as a helicopter pilot with the RAF's Search and Rescue Force. He is now based at RAF Valley on Anglesey, where he will remain with No. 22 Squadron until 2013, working aboard Sea King helicopters. His first rescue mission in October 2010, as co-pilot, was to an off-shore gas rig in Morecambe Bay to airlift a sick man to hospital on the mainland.

WORKING
FOR CHARITY

William has never forgotten that 500 representatives of charities supported by his mother, Diana, Princess of Wales, walked behind her coffin as it was borne to Westminster Abbey for her funeral. The Princess had encouraged both her sons to help those in need as has their father, the Prince of Wales. Prince William has followed his parents' example, becoming patron or president of 19 charities, often leading the way by taking part in fund-raising events.

He and Harry had been taken by their mother on visits to Centrepoint and also to shelters for those suffering from HIV/AIDS. William remembered these visits when he took on patronage of Centrepoint, the charity for young homeless people, proving his commitment by sleeping rough near Blackfriars Bridge in London on a freezing December night.

Left: The Prince meets young people at a Centrepoint venue in central London, in December 2009. Centrepoint is a charity formed to improve the lives of homeless young people.

William and Catherine's wedding in April 2011 has directly benefited 26 charities. The couple set up the Royal Wedding Charitable Gift Fund, asking that donations should be made in lieu of wedding presents. So far more than one million pounds has been received, much of which has already been distributed to the charities.

Left: William and Harry worked at a Red Cross depot in Bristol to help pack supplies for tsunami victims in January 2005.

Above: The Princes played a charity polo match at the Longdole Polo Club, Birdlip, Gloucestershire to raise money for those affected by the Indian tsunami.

Above: The Sports Relief run in London in 2004 saw Prince William race to raise money for needy people around the world.

Both Princes responded quickly to the devastating Asian tsunami of 2004, raising £40,000 for survivors by playing in a charity polo match just days after the event. A week later they volunteered at a British Red Cross distribution centre, making up aid packages for those hit by the disaster.

While on his gap year, William undertook work experience at the children's unit at the Royal Marsden Hospital, Chelsea, and soon became a patron of the institution.

He is also a patron of Mountain Rescue England and Wales, and of the African-based Tusk Trust which works to conserve wildlife and help with community development across the continent. His first official duty with the charity was in 2007, when he launched a 5,000-mile (8,000-km) bike ride across Africa.

Two years later, in November 2009, he and his brother set up the Charitable Foundation of Prince William and Prince Harry to provide grants to needy young people, wounded servicemen and women, and for sustainable development, both at home and overseas. William also supports Sentebale, the charity set up jointly by his brother Harry and Prince Seeiso of Lesotho to help orphans and vulnerable children in the Southern African country.

Sport is high on Prince William's agenda and he has raised money through activities such as polo and charity runs with teams from Sandhurst and Clarence House to boost the coffers of Sports Relief. He is also patron of the English Schools' Swimming Association.

Since his marriage, Prince William and his wife Catherine, Duchess of Cambridge, have attended charity events at home and abroad, a clear signal that they intend to continue supporting good causes.

A ROYAL
ENGAGEMENT

The announcement that came out of the blue on a dull November day in 2010 swept all other news off television screens and front pages of newspapers. Prince William and his long-term girlfriend Catherine Middleton were to marry.

No matter that Catherine was not of royal blood. This was love and the world could see it. Private joy and public hope surrounded the proceedings as the couple walked together into the red and gold splendour of the Entrée Room at St James's Palace to face the world's media. On Catherine's left hand shone the glorious sapphire and diamond ring that once belonged to William's mother, the late Diana, Princess of Wales.

William revealed that he had taken the ring with him, safely tucked into a pocket in his rucksack, when he had proposed to Catherine a few weeks earlier in Africa on the shores of Lake Rutundu, high on the slopes of Mount Kenya.

Catherine and William had known each other for nine years, growing closer as time went on. The news of their engagement came as a happy surprise. Catherine, facing her first formal public appearance with her fiancé, coped naturally and confidently with the media attention. She admitted that the prospect of joining the Royal Family and living constantly under public scrutiny was daunting but revealed that William was giving her the help and support she needed. 'William is a great teacher,' she said. 'Hopefully, I'll take it in my stride.'

The dry humour of the Prince of Wales, William's father, came to the fore when he was asked to comment on his son's engagement to Catherine. He said that he was thrilled, adding: 'They've been practising long enough.' His wife, the Duchess of Cornwall, was equally forthright: 'I'm just so happy and so are they. It's wicked!' she told reporters.

Left: Prince William and Catherine Middleton announce their engagement to the world on 16 November 2010, at St James's Palace.

Right: The smiling couple pose for the photographers, Catherine wearing her sapphire and diamond engagement ring that once belonged to Princess Diana.

Catherine's future grandmother-in-law, Her Majesty The Queen, expressed delight in an official statement and privately admitted the news was 'brilliant', saying that it had taken the couple 'a very long time'.

Catherine's parents, Carole and Michael Middleton, who had clearly already taken William to their hearts, said their future son-in-law was 'wonderful' and that they were extremely fond of him.

William revealed that he had waited for a time to propose to Catherine because he knew the pressures of royal life; he wanted to give her the chance to 'see what happens on the other side' and to back out if it all became too much. Catherine saw the other side and, fortunately, she liked it. William was happy that she would cope. 'It's about making your own future and your own destiny and Kate will do a very good job of that,' he said.

WILLIAM THE
BRIDEGROOM

The whole of Britain came to a standstill on 29 April 2011 when Prince William, the new Duke of Cambridge, married his long-time love, Catherine Middleton. The chosen venue, Westminster Abbey, with its sweeping arches, the highest Gothic nave in the country, and with a royal connection stretching back to the 11th century, was filled with a romance and magic for this wedding of two popular young people that touched every one of the 2,000 guests.

A fresh green avenue of trees and informal arrangements of white spring flowers gave a sense of rustic simplicity, tempering the high majesty of the occasion. Almost one million people lined the route from Buckingham Palace to the Abbey, to be part of the splendour and pageantry of the royal wedding. Those near the Abbey cheered when a claret-coloured Bentley drew up bearing the bridegroom William, and his best man Prince Harry. The brothers, William, his Garter Sash a vivid blue across his scarlet tunic, which also bore his RAF Wings, the Garter Star and Golden Jubilee Medal and Harry, wearing his formal Blues and Royals officer's uniform, were greeted by the Dean of Westminster. As they made their way inside, Prince William stopped to greet friends, with a special word for his uncle Charles Spencer, the ninth Earl Spencer, brother of his late mother Princess Diana.

William waited, resplendent in his uniform of Colonel of the Irish Guards, as the Choir sang the opening lines of Charles Parry's soaring anthem *I Was Glad*. Catherine, radiant and lovely, her arm on that of her father's, moved slowly along the crimson carpet to meet her bridegroom at the High Altar. As she reached his side, William gazed at her and whispered: 'You look beautiful.'

The Bishop of London, the Right Reverend and Right Honourable Dr Richard Chartres, who has known William since he was a child, gave the address, telling the couple: 'Be who God meant you to be and you will set the world on fire' – words of the bride's namesake, St Catherine of Sienna.

As William and Catherine, with a prompt from the Archbishop of Canterbury, the Most Reverend and Right Honourable Dr Rowan Williams, made their vows, William, after a brief struggle, slipped the wedding ring, made from Welsh gold, on to his bride's finger. The newly-weds emerged from Westminster Abbey to the ringing cheers of a million well-wishers, many of whom had been waiting for hours. It was a day of perfect pageantry but also a family day, when traditional British reserve broke down and friendship and love brought home the real meaning of a wedding.

Right: Prince William, with his best man Prince Harry, arrives at Westminster Abbey on 29 April 2011 for his wedding to Catherine Middleton.

Left: Before the Archbishop of Canterbury, Prince William and Catherine Middleton, the Duke and Duchess of Cambridge, make their wedding vows.

Above: The happy couple, now man and wife, walk together through the door of Westminster Abbey into the sunshine, after their wedding ceremony.

Below: More than one million well-wishers lined the streets of London to catch a glimpse of the royal newly-weds.

AT HOME &
AT WORK

After their wedding, the Duke and Duchess of Cambridge slipped away for a quiet weekend together, rather than flying off on an exotic honeymoon. Although they did take a honeymoon in the Seychelles a few weeks later, both William and Catherine seem to relish a simple life at home in each other's company.

Their main home is a white-washed rented farmhouse, hidden away down a winding lane in Anglesey in Wales. With wonderful views over Snowdonia and a private beach, the cottage offers the seclusion that William and Catherine enjoy.

Their home is not far from RAF Valley, where William, known as Flight Lieutenant William Wales, works as a co-pilot with C Flight, 22 Squadron, flying Sea King Search and Rescue helicopters. When they are not travelling on official duties and visits, William leaves home early in the morning to undertake his flying duties, while Catherine looks after the house. Just a few days after their wedding, the new Duke of Cambridge was part of the team which rescued a retired High Court

Both William and Catherine understand the importance of a happy family life. During the years they have been together, they have grown to know each other's families and it is clear that the families themselves enjoy each other's company. This was apparent over the August bank holiday in 2011, when William and Catherine and her parents, Carole and Michael Middleton, were invited to a family gathering with the Prince of Wales and the Duchess of Cornwall at Birkhall, Prince Charles's Scottish retreat.

Left: 'Will Wales' waits to greet his grandmother Her Majesty The Queen, in April 2011 before she and the Duke of Edinburgh visited RAF Valley.

Right: The day after their wedding, the Duke and Duchess of Cambridge walk hand-in-hand from Buckingham Palace before leaving by helicopter for a secret destination.

judge who had suffered a heart attack while walking in Snowdonia. The same day his helicopter sped to the rescue of four other climbers who had found themselves in trouble in mountainous terrain.

Off duty, the couple socialize with friends, go out for a meal in the local pub or visit the cinema. Both enjoy sport, and they keep fit by running or taking a walk along the beach, and William plays football when he can. They have a lot to share. They laugh together, teasing each other gently. They have a circle of good friends in whose company they know they can relax and enjoy a normal social life. In London, they enjoy privacy in an apartment at St James's Palace.

Above: The Prince, a level-headed and brave helicopter pilot, disembarks from a Sea King helicopter during a training exercise at Holyhead Mountain, Anglesey, in March 2011.

JOINING
'THE FIRM'

Senior members of the Royal Family know that they have a job to do, referring to themselves as 'The Firm' – a term first used by The Queen's father King George VI.

That job is to be seen supporting British enterprise, industry, society and community at home and abroad. The newest partnership within The Firm is that of William and Catherine – he brought up in the tradition of public service, she a newcomer, albeit one who seems born to the job.

Their first public engagement together, before their marriage, was on a chilly February day in Trearddur Bay, near their home in Anglesey, North Wales. Catherine, wrapped warmly in a chocolate-trimmed camel coat, smashed a bottle of champagne on the bows of a new inflatable boat and the couple joined the team at the RNLI station for a service of dedication. Later, they visited the New Zealand High Commission in London to sign the book of condolence for those who had lost their lives in the terrible earthquake that hit the city of Christchurch.

Left: The Duke and Duchess of Cambridge attend Canada Day celebrations at Parliament Hill, Ottawa, on their highly successful North American tour, in July 2011.

The Duke of Cambridge and his wife were allowed to enjoy a few hours of quiet time together during their busy trip to Canada. They paddled their own canoe to uninhabited Eagle Island in Blachford Lake where they dined on caribou steaks, bannock bread and cranberries before watching the slow setting of the midnight sun. The three-hour escape was William's idea, so that he and his wife could enjoy a break from the round of official engagements.

Right: The royal couple enjoy a visit to the Calgary Stampede to watch cowboy activities.

Below right: The Duke and Duchess were stars of the evening at the 'Brits to Watch' event at the Belasco Theatre in Los Angeles, California in July 2011.

A surprise visit to Belfast in early March enlivened the Shrove Tuesday celebrations as both William and Catherine proved more than adept when they joined in a street pancake-tossing race. A week later, William travelled alone to commiserate with the people of Australia and New Zealand who had suffered, respectively, extraordinary flooding and a massive, destructive earthquake.

But it was their official visit to Canada, where they joined hundreds of thousands of locals celebrating Canada Day, that proved a real triumph. William and Catherine, smiling, relaxed and happy, charmed a nation. They met sick children and cancer patients, taking time to talk to them, they enjoyed a rock concert and, wearing cream cowboy hats, they were the toast of the Calgary Stampede, where they watched the rodeo stars of the future and saw fearless cowboys wrestle huge steers to the ground. After Canada the couple made a short visit to Los Angeles, where they were welcomed by Hollywood stars, and where William, president of the British Academy of Film and Television Arts (BAFTA), supported British talent in the field of film and television.

THE
FUTURE

rince William, Duke of Cambridge will one day be King. His training for this most elevated and demanding of roles began almost from the moment he was born. With Catherine, Duchess of Cambridge at his side, his will be a modern monarchy, on which the hopes of the British people ride. William's upbringing has brought him closely into contact with British citizens. His time at university and in the RAF has been a great leveller, helping him to understand the hopes, fears and everyday concerns of ordinary working people. His enthusiasms – for sport, modern culture, music and cinema – are those shared by his future subjects. He has his mother's charm and ability to communicate easily with everybody. Although he was brought up in the rarefied atmosphere of Palace life, both his parents saw that he took part in everyday activities that all children and young people enjoy.

He is intelligent, perceptive and has a maturity born of experience, which will stand him in good stead when on that future day he dons the crimson velvet Robe of State and is crowned Monarch of the United Kingdom.

Right: The Duke and Duchess of Cambridge, smiling together for photographers in Santa Barbara, California.